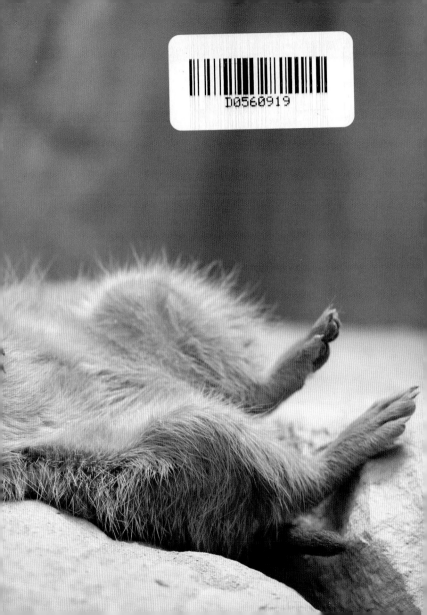

WISDOM

of

MEERKATS

Art Director: Brian MacMullen
Designer: Neil Dvorak
Editor: Rachael Lanicci
Photo Researcher: Benjamin DeWalt

Metro Books
122 Fifth Avenue
New York, NY 10011

ISBN: 978-1-4351-0535-5

Printed and bound in China

3 5 7 9 10 8 6 4 2

WISDOM

— *of* —

MEERKATS

Compiled by
Rachael Lanicci

METRO BOOKS
NEW YORK

"We are **made** for loving.
If we don't love,
we will be like
plants without water."

–Archbishop Desmond Tutu

'Life's like a boom-a- rang. The more good

you throw out, the more you get in return."

–*Josh S. Hinds*

"Every time you **smile**
at someone, it is an action
of **love**, a **gift** to that person,
a **beautiful** thing."

–*Mother Teresa*

"Change is never easy."

–Sally Field

"A part of kindness consists in **loving** people **more** than they deserve."

–Joseph Joubert

"That is what **friendship** means. **Sharing** the prejudice of experience."

–Charles Bukowski

"Memory is the mother of **all wisdom.**"

–*Aeschylus*

"No act of **kindness**, however small, is **ever** wasted."

–Aesop

"No matter how hard the loss, defeat might **serve as well** as victory to **shake the soul** and **let the glory out.**"

–*Al Gore*

"In the **hopes** of reaching the moon, men fail to see the **flowers** that blossom at their feet."

–Albert Schweitzer

"Happiness is where we find it,
but rarely where we seek it."

–J. Petit Senn

"Go **confidently** in the direction of your dreams. **Live** the life you have **imagined.**"

–Henry David Thoreau

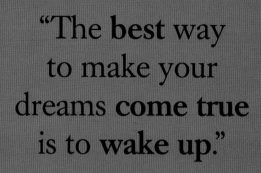

"The **best** way
to make your
dreams **come true**
is to **wake up**."

–Paul Valéry

"If you put your mind to it, you can accomplish **anything**."

–Robert Zemeckis

"**Do not follow**
where the path may lead.
Go instead where
there is no path
and **leave a trail.**"

–Harold R. McAlindon

"The **only** job where you start at the top is digging a hole."

–*Anonymous*

"What **counts** is not necessarily the size of the dog in the fight—it's the **size** of the **fight** in the **dog**."

–*Dwight D. Eisenhower*

"A **smile** is a curve that sets **everything** straight."

–Anonymous

"Joy is the feeling of grinning inside."

–*Melba Colgrove*

"To unpathed waters,
undreamed shores."

–*William Shakespeare*

"People are like stained-glass windows. They **sparkle and shine** when the sun is out, but when the darkness sets in, their **true beauty** is revealed only if there is a **light from within.**"

–*Elisabeth Kübler-Ross*

"Think of all the beauty still

around you and **be happy.**"

–Anne Frank

"Everything has **beauty**, but not everyone sees it."

–*Confucius*

"To love and be loved
is to feel the sun
from both sides."

–*David Viscott*

"The **best** things
in life
aren't things."

–Art Buchwald

"Experience is the name everyone gives ...

... to their **mistakes**."

–*Oscar Wilde*

"Waste not fresh **tears**
over old
griefs."

–Euripides

"Imagination is the

eye of the soul."

–Joseph Joubert

"The right way is not always the popular and easy way. **Standing for right** when it is unpopular is a true test of **moral character.**"

–*Margaret Chase Smith*

"Real **glory** springs from the silent **conquest** of ourselves."

–Anonymous

"We are all **artists**; some of us just have yet to find our medium."

–*Herb Green*

"The foolish man
seeks **happiness**
in the distance,
the **wise** grows it
under his feet."

–*James Oppenheim*

"The **brave** man is not he who does not feel afraid, but he who **conquers that fear.**"

–*Nelson Mandela*

"He who treads
the path of **love** walks
a thousand meters
as if it were only one."

–Japanese proverb

"Life shrinks or expands
in proportion
to one's
courage."

–*Anaïs Nin*

"The best way
to **find yourself**
is to lose yourself
in the **service**
of others."

–Gandhi

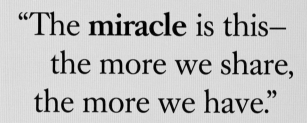

"The **miracle** is this—
the more we share,
the more we have."

–Leonard Nimoy

"A **real** friend is one who walks in when the rest of the world walks out."

–*Walter Winchell*

"A man sees in the world what he carries in his heart."

–*Goethe*

"If you tell the **truth,**
you don't have to
remember anything."

–*Mark Twain*

"Wisdom is not a product of schooling but of the lifelong attempt to acquire it."

–Albert Einstein

"One of the things
I keep **learning** is
that the **secret of being
happy** is **doing things for
other people.**"

–*Dick Gregory*

"Minds are like parachutes; they only function when open."

–*Thomas Dewar*

"Man is a **universe** within himself."

–*Bob Marley*

"We **all** have courage,
even if we have to
dig a little to **find** it."

–Tori Amos

"Never measure the height of a mountain until you have reached the top. Then you will see how low it was."

–*Dag Hammarskjöld*

"Love is a friendship
set to music."

–Joseph Campbell

"**Always** do right—this will **gratify** some and **astonish** the rest."

–*Mark Twain*

"If you **stand straight**, do not fear a crooked shadow."

–Chinese proverb

"The scars you acquire by exercising **courage** will **never** make you feel inferior."

–D. A. Battista

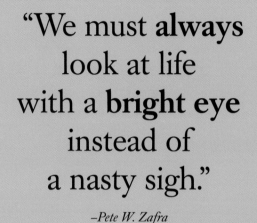

"We must **always** look at life with a **bright eye** instead of a nasty sigh."

–*Pete W. Zafra*

"For me,

the **safest** place is **out on a limb.**"

–Shirley MacLaine

"The only way around

is through."

–Robert Frost

"The harder you fall . . . . . . the **higher** you bounce."

–Anonymous

"Sleep is the best meditation."

–Dalai Lama

"Friendship doubles joy

and halves grief."

– *Anonymous*

"Life can only be understood backwards; but it must be lived forwards."

–*Søren Kierkegaard*

PICTURE CREDITS